Jackie -
May God grant
you many more years
of Christmas Blessings
and Memories.

Joyce

TWILA PARIS
WITH JEANIE PRICE

Making a Christmas Memory

Photography by
Robert McKendrick
Styling by
Cindy Meissner

Tyndale House Publishers, Inc.
WHEATON, ILLINOIS

Very special thanks to . . .
Franki Black for a wonderful idea;
Mary Lydia, Oren, Inez, and Starla Paris,
   and to Mary, Cynthia, Cody, and Matthew
   Wright for generously contributing time,
   talent, and thought to this project;
the entire Paris and Wright families for all
   the warm Christmas memories;
Jeanie Price for capturing the vision so
   eloquently;
and to our Lord Jesus Christ — whom we
   celebrate!

Victorian postcards on cover and p. 35
courtesy of Billy Graham Center Museum.
Dickens's volumes on p. 4 courtesy of Wheaton
College Archives and Special Collections.

Unless otherwise indicated, Scripture verses are
from *The Living Bible,* copyright © 1971 owned by
assignment by KNT Charitable Trust. All rights
reserved.

CONTENTS

A Letter from Twila   PAGE 5

ONE   A Gift of Family   PAGE 7

TWO   A Gift of Celebration   PAGE 21

THREE   A Gift of Worship   PAGE 33

FOUR   A Gift of Praise   PAGE 39

A LETTER FROM TWILA

Dear Friends:

An enduring fantasy, common to people of all cultures, is that there is a flawless and ideal way in which any special event or occasion should be celebrated or conducted. Usually this vision of perfection is based on the shaky foundations of legend, imagination, and "we've always done it that way."

This seems to be especially true of Christmas. No other holiday or special event is so surrounded by idealism and expectations. In fact, in the minds of many the only two people who have ever truly celebrated the Christmas season were a nineteenth-century novelist named Dickens and a twentieth-century songwriter named Berlin. Everyone else has fallen short of experiencing a merry Christmas.

Unfortunately, by establishing such high and unrealistic expectations, we set ourselves up for disappointment. Eventually, the most holy season of the year — the celebration of the birth of our Lord —

becomes little more than an exhausting effort in indulgence.

The purpose of this book is to challenge you to make your Christmas a meaningful experience rather than a time of hollow and empty busyness. The Christmas season ought to be an occasion when Christians strive to share and experience the joy and hope of Christ with their family, acquaintances, and friends; when Christians dare to open their hearts and homes with love and generosity.

Years from now, when you think back on this and other Christmases, my hope is that your memories will not be filled with endless activities designed to bring about some vague and cloudy ideal. Rather, I hope your memories are of times devoted to celebrating the love of friends and family, the love of Christ, and the true meaning of Christmas.

With Love,
Twila

ONE

A Gift of Family

THE HERITAGE of the Paris family is one of service and devotion to our Lord. My earliest memories are filled with stories of relatives who have dedicated their lives to bringing the good news of salvation to a hungry world.

Perhaps this is why Christmas has always been a special time in my family. This wonderful season is an occasion when we can enjoy the support of those whose love for each other is unconditional and whose vision is blind to flaws and weaknesses. It's also a time when we can let our hair down and act silly.

As you read, notice that it's not the presents or the fancy meals that have endured through time. Instead, it's the small gestures and the heartfelt expressions of love that have filled the scrapbook of these special family reunions.

Take time out this Christmas to show everyone in your family how much they mean to you. When you give yourself away, you offer a gift that continues to provide joy and happiness long after the needles have fallen off the tree and the sleigh bells are lying silent in the attic.

Peeking into Santa's Workshop

Stature is not always measured in such mundane terms as physical size or personal wealth. One of the most important and larger-than-life men I have ever known stood barely five and a half feet tall. He possessed no temporal riches — except for the countless people who considered him their friend. Yet his abundant kindness and compassion generated a spirit of love that made him seem like a giant to those whose lives he touched. That man was my Grandfather Paris.

I have always felt that my grandfather's life was especially blessed because he, like our Lord, was both a pastor and a carpenter. I still remember how the same hands that could turn a pile of boards and nails into a sturdy porch or a graceful sleigh could also compose a moving sermon or baptize a new Christian.

Perhaps the most cherished memory I have of this great man happened a few weeks before one of my earliest Christmases. Over a quiet breakfast, Grandfather Paris announced in a casual way that he had an important project he needed to complete. He turned to me and explained in the sternest voice he could muster that I should remain in the house so as not to disturb him.

Well, naturally this only served to fuel my youthful imagination and curiosity. So after

9

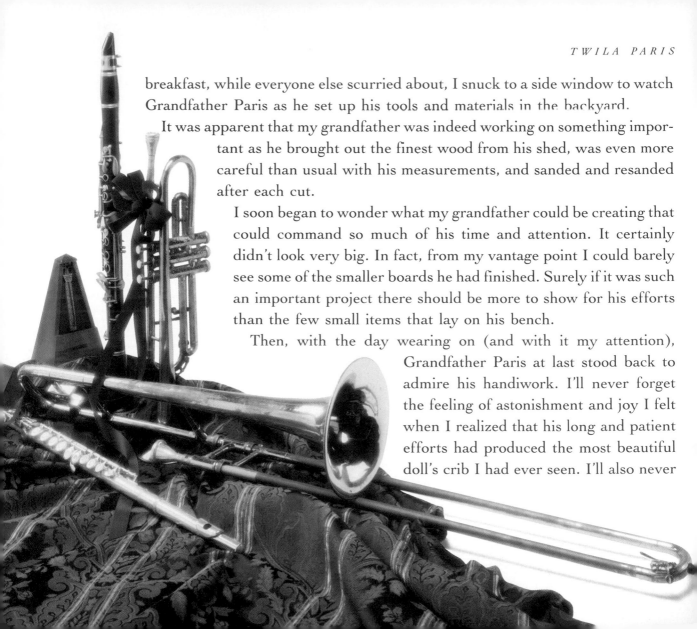

breakfast, while everyone else scurried about, I snuck to a side window to watch Grandfather Paris as he set up his tools and materials in the backyard.

It was apparent that my grandfather was indeed working on something important as he brought out the finest wood from his shed, was even more careful than usual with his measurements, and sanded and resanded after each cut.

I soon began to wonder what my grandfather could be creating that could command so much of his time and attention. It certainly didn't look very big. In fact, from my vantage point I could barely see some of the smaller boards he had finished. Surely if it was such an important project there should be more to show for his efforts than the few small items that lay on his bench.

Then, with the day wearing on (and with it my attention), Grandfather Paris at last stood back to admire his handiwork. I'll never forget the feeling of astonishment and joy I felt when I realized that his long and patient efforts had produced the most beautiful doll's crib I had ever seen. I'll also never forget the endless days of waiting for Christmas morning when at last I could play with this wonderful present. (Believe me, patience is more than a virtue for a two-year-old. It's almost an impossibility.)

As an adult, when I think about this gesture of love from my grandfather I realize anew what it is that makes Christmas special. Just as a gentle man lovingly crafted a toy for his granddaughter to show her how very special she was to him, so, too, did God lovingly send his Son as a flawless living sacrifice to express his infinite love for us.

Musical instruments share one quality with the musicians who create their innumerable "voices": they each have a singular, distinguishing personality. For instance, the waves of majestic tones produced by the pipe organ create a solemn air that is as distinct from the airy notes of a flute as the bark of a Marine drill sergeant is from the recitation of a poet.

If you were asked to identify which group of instruments reflect the personality of a town crier, the chances are you would choose the brass family. Whether your favorite music is classical or big band, you know something exciting is about to happen when the conductor points to the horn section.

Perhaps it was with this in mind that, as children, my father, Oren Paris, and his brother Leland would awaken their parents every Christmas morning at 4:00 A.M. with a rousing medley of carols on the trumpet and trombone. In my family, the

Hark, the Herald Trombones Sing

wait for Christmas morning has always revolved on a 365-day cycle. It's appropriate then that my father and uncle should herald the most important day of the year by pursing their lips, taking a deep breath, and blowing with all their might.

The rafters stopped shaking long ago at my father's boyhood home as both he and my uncle have since made more "mature" use of their years of music lessons. I think they would both admit that their boyish exuberance was based more on a desire to see what packages lay behind my grandparent's carved manger scene than an effort to celebrate what those lovely carvings represented.

Still, there's something appropriate about abandoning restraint when it comes to announcing Christmas morning. The biblical account of our Savior's birth illustrates on both an angelic and a human level that the entrance of the King of kings into his earthly kingdom was cause for pageantry and celebration.

This is not to say that quiet reflection and prayerful meditation are not appropriate responses to this holy day. Indeed, Christmas should be a time when we acknowledge the wonderful gift God gave us in his Son. But a day like Christmas demands a variety of responses — and one of these is unpacking whatever instruments have been hiding in our attics since high school (or even grabbing our most resonant pots and pans) and raising a cacophony of joy to the heavens, announcing that Jesus Christ, the Lamb of God, was born in a manger two thousand years ago and lives today in heaven and in our hearts.

Despite seasonal editorials by professional cynics and modern-day Scrooges, Christmas really does bring out the best in people. It's the one time of year when everyone seems to take seriously the adage that it's better to give than to receive. Especially when it comes to entertainment.

With Christmas TV specials, the annual run of *The Nutcracker Suite* at the local theater, and neighborhood carolers, Christmas can cause sensory overload. The sad thing is that Christmas is often the single occasion when families get together. Yet, instead of simply basking in the loving glow of those we care about most, we allow others to monopolize our precious time together.

My husband's family has found a solution for this problem. They have a wonderful forty-year tradition that brings everyone closer and provides hours of entertainment. Each year the youngest members of the family create a play that they then perform on Christmas Day. Preparations are exhaustive, covering everything from costumes to seating assignments.

One year, my nephews Cody and Matthew wrote a musical called *The Wonderful Present*. It demonstrates what a little initiative and a lot of cooperation can achieve. I am offering *The Wonderful Present* as

a play your family can enjoy this year to introduce them to the exciting world of theater production. I have included the program notes of the original cast and crew to give proper credit, but be sure to modify these to fit your family.

Although this musical was written by and for children, consider including other members of your family for future productions. Since the youngest members will perform this play, you might give the honor of the next year's performance to the eldest. You might also try putting various people together who don't know each other very well or don't spend much time together, like in-laws or the teenage boys and the grade-school girls. By doing this you will help nurture budding relationships and enhance those relationships that have stood the test of time.

The Wonderful Present

BY CODY AND MATTHEW WRIGHT

THE CAST
Edwin Crownover: Cody Wright; *Anne Crownover:* Susannah Wright; *Richard Crownover:* Matthew Wright; *Robert Crownover:* David Wright; *Jonathan Crownover:* Joshua Wright

THE CREW
Stage Director: Cody Wright; *Stage Manager:* Matthew Wright; *Costume Designer:* David Wright; *Choreographer:* Joshua Wright; *Lighting Designer:* Anita Bone; *Sound Director:* Anita Bone; *Program Cover Design:* Cynthia Wright

THE TIME: Sometime in the mid-twentieth century; THE SETTING: Living room of the Crownover's home

(As the play begins, Edwin is sitting on the couch. The telephone rings.)

Edwin: Hello? . . . Oh, hello, Father. . . . You do? . . . Not again. . . . How long this time? . . . Oh dear. Well, don't worry about us. We'll be fine. . . . Yes, we'll miss you, too. . . . I will. Good-bye.

(Richard, Robert, and Anne enter.)

Anne: Edwin, why do you look so sad?
Edwin: Please sit down. Father just called from the train station. He was called away suddenly on business and won't be back for two weeks.

> **Robert:** Not again! Not at Christmas. Especially this year. . . . Mother is still not feeling any better and worrying about Father will only make her feel worse.
> **Edwin:** I know, but we all need to be as supportive as

possible. Father wouldn't leave if he didn't have to, and Mother needs an extra dose of our love.
Anne: We should all work together to cheer up Mother so that she won't worry about Father. If we work hard at encouraging her, maybe she will be well enough to come downstairs for Christmas morning.

(There is a knock at the door. Richard answers it and lets Jonathan in.)

Richard: Hello, Jonathan. Come on in. Let me take your coat.

(Richard takes Jonathan's coat and hangs it in the closet.)

Jonathan: Hello, everyone. I came by to see how your mother is doing.
Richard: We're hoping she will be well enough by Christmas to come downstairs and celebrate with us. We were just thinking of some things we could do to encourage her.
Edwin: I know. Let's practice the Christmas music we will be singing in the church choir this Sunday. Mother always says it's hard to have a heavy heart when we lift it in song to God.

Anne: That's a great idea. I'll run up and open Mother's bedroom door so she can hear us better.

(Anne disappears offstage. Edwin, Richard, Robert, and Jonathan stand in a semicircle. Anne comes back and joins them.)

Robert: Let's start with "Silent Night."

(Everyone sings "Silent Night.")

Richard: Look, everyone! *(points to audience)* There's a group of carolers assembling on our lawn. I'll go turn the porch light on.

(Richard turns to leave just as the phone rings.)

Anne: I'll get it. Hello? . . . Oh, Father, it's so good to hear your voice. We wish you could be with us this Christmas. . . . What? You are? . . . Everyone will be so excited! . . . Yes, we love you too! *(hangs up phone and turns to others)* Hey, everyone! Father's coming home after all! He said it's more important to be with those he loves at Christmas than to be anywhere else.

(Richard has returned in time to hear the good news.)

Richard: It's going to be a merry Christmas after all.
Anne: I'll go tell Mother.

(Anne exits and then goes into the audience to hand out the words to "Away in a Manger.")

Richard: Listen everyone. Can you hear the carolers?

(Audience sings "Away in a Manger.")

(Anne returns.)

Anne: Mother was so happy to hear the good news that she said she's feeling better already.
Richard: God has given us a wonderful gift this Christmas: each other.

(Everyone, including the audience, sings "Joy to the World.")

(The cast leaves the stage to hug members of the audience and say, "Merry Christmas!")

Perhaps no other time of the year is as closely associated with special memories as the Christmas season. Yet, while most of our time and energy is devoted to shopping for presents, it's not the gifts we receive that we talk about over and over again. Usually it's the little events — the things that seemed insignificant when they happened — that make us smile each time they are told. Let me share with you just a few of these momentous minor occasions that my family loves to relive each Christmas.

My husband, Jack, never tires of recalling the manner in which his father, Jack, Sr., taught him how to share the true meaning of Christmas with others. Each year they would make a list of the neediest families in their small Arkansas community. They would then take this list, along with several carts of toys they had purchased together, to the local grocer the week before Christmas.

The families on the list always came to that store to buy groceries. This time, though, when they would bring their baskets of supplies for Christmas dinner to the cash register, the grocer would ring them up as usual, and, to their disbelief, he would refuse to take their money. He would simply tell them that their bill already had been paid in full by a secret benefactor. He would then give each child in the family a toy. At the end of the holiday season, the grocer would total the receipts and give them to Jack's father, who would pay whatever was owed.

When I was six years old, my family spent Christmas with a group of missionaries in Venezuela. Because there were no fir trees available, let alone shiny glass ornaments, we decided to participate in a local custom by decorating a tree branch with colored tissue paper and then prayerfully dedicating it to our friends and their work. I have since seen many beautiful Christmas trees, including the massive specimens that grace our nation's capital each year. But none hold as special a place in my heart as that little stick we wrapped in paper and dedicated to the tremendous work to which our hosts had dedicated their lives.

Sometimes memories serve to fuel the creation of other memories. I don't know if we were inspired by *It's a Wonderful Life* or just by the spirit of the season, but several years ago my home church created a game called "Angels and Mortals." Because some of my family's fondest memories have resulted from this game, we now play it each year.

Unlike most games, anyone who plays "Angels and Mortals" is a winner. The rules are simple: We put each one's name on a slip of paper and then place the names in a hat. Each person draws a name and becomes that person's "secret angel."

Over the course of the holiday season, each "angel" must secretly do nice things for his or her "mortal." At the end of the holidays we have a party and tell each other who our mortal was. In addition to being great fun, this game gives us a sense of just how thankful we should be for the unseen things real angels do for us each day.

As a romantic gesture in honor of the first gift he gave her on their first date, my Grandfather Paris always gave my Grandmother Paris a box of chocolate-covered cherries for Christmas. And every year my grandmother would open her one present from my grandfather and exclaim with joy that once again she had gotten exactly what she wanted and what she had looked forward to receiving since the previous year.

My grandfather passed away before Christmas several years ago and in an effort to help ease my grandmother's sorrow, her sons bought her a box of chocolate-covered cherries. As she had done for so many years, my grandmother opened her gift and expressed sincere appreciation for this tasty reminder of her first date. This loving exchange went on for eight years, until one day my grandmother told my sister Starla in private that she had never really cared for chocolate-covered cherries but had eaten them so as not to hurt anyone's feelings! When my father and uncle heard this revelation, they did the only honorable thing good sons could do — they continued to buy my grandmother her box of chocolate-covered cherries each Christmas.

We have since laughed many times about how my grandmother didn't express her love for her husband in such common ways as fixing grand meals or wearing his favorite perfume. Instead, she lovingly ate the one thing that made her tastebuds cringe: chocolate-covered cherries.

As your family puts together a scrapbook of memories over the years, don't forget the small things are the most important. After all, if it hadn't been for the birth of a tiny baby in a remote part of the world two thousand years ago, there would be no season in which to build our joyous remembrances.

TWO

A Gift of Celebration

CHRISTMAS MORNING BRUNCH

Hot Coffee and Tea
Fresh Orange and Grapefruit Slices
Egg Casserole
Coffee Cake
Homemade Waffles
Icebox French Bread

In ANCIENT times, the common meal was an active symbol of peace and harmony between two parties. Today, family meals evidence similar affinity by demonstrating the ties of love and honor we share through our common heritage.

Some meals, of course, have more significance than others. Sunday dinners, Independence Day picnics, and birthday celebrations each summon Norman Rockwell-types of images of joyful gatherings and overflowing tables. Christmas meals, especially, are times of jubilation and should be given the same attentiveness as a fine restaurant gives its most valued customers.

Each Christmas my sister-in-law, Cynthia Wright, prepares a wonderful morning brunch and an even more impressive evening dinner. The recipes on the following pages are from one of Cynthia's recent Christmas extravaganzas. I have included some of her comments (and some fascinating historical and biblical lore) since so much of what she prepares has spiritual significance in addition to providing sensory pleasure.

This is my favorite Christmas morning menu. Everything is fresh and made from scratch, yet much of it can be prepared on Christmas Eve. Together, these recipes should serve at least twelve people (depending, of course, on whether everyone's priority is appetites or presents).

COFFEE CAKE

4 cups flour
1/2 cup shortening
1/2 cup butter
3 tablespoons sugar
1 teaspoon salt
1 cup warm milk
1 tablespoon yeast
3 eggs

ICING:
1/2 cup powdered sugar
1/2 cup butter
1/4 cup cream

FILLING:
1/2 stick soft butter
3 cups nuts
2 cups raisins
2 cups brown sugar and
white sugar, mixed
4 tablespoons cinnamon

Dissolve yeast in the warm milk. In another bowl, mix first five ingredients until they resemble a pie crust. Add milk, yeast, and eggs. Allow dough to rise for 20 minutes. Roll out dough on a pastry board and spread with filling. Roll dough into a large roll with filling in the center. Let rise until light to the touch. Preheat oven to 400°. Bake for 20-25 minutes. Spread icing evenly over top of bread. Let cool for about 10 minutes. Slice and serve.

HOMEMADE WAFFLES

1 egg
1 cup whipping cream
1 cup milk
2 cups cake flour
½ cup sugar

4 tablespoons baking
* powder*
¼ teaspoon salt
¼ cup melted butter

Heat waffle iron. Beat egg, then add cream and milk. Sift dry ingredients together and add to egg, cream, and milk mixture. Beat with rotary beater while adding melted butter. Bake about 5 minutes in center of hot waffle iron.

ICEBOX FRENCH BREAD

¼ cup cornmeal
2¼ cups warm water
2 packages yeast
½ cup sugar

2 tablespoons butter
1 tablespoon salt
6 cups flour
Cornmeal

Mix all ingredients with mixer. Place on a floured cutting board and allow to rest for 20 minutes. Shape into two separate loaves. Slit top of each loaf and sprinkle with cornmeal. Leave in refrigerator overnight.

On Christmas morning, preheat oven to 425°. Bake for 25 minutes. Spray bread with water every 10 minutes for a crusty finish.

EGG CASSEROLE

16 eggs
16 ounces grated monterey jack cheese
2 medium cans hot green chilies
16 ounces cottage cheese
¼ cup flour
½ teaspoon baking powder

Preheat oven to 350°. Beat eggs. Add remaining ingredients. Pour mixture into lightly greased 9 × 14-inch pan and bake for 45 minutes.

As you prepare your Christmas meal, don't think of it only as a time to nourish your physical self. Instead, recognize and celebrate

CHRISTMAS DINNER

BEVERAGE
Sparkling Cider

APPETIZERS
Artichoke Parmesan • Hot Brie • Scalloped Oysters

MAIN MEAL
Twenty-Four-Hour Salad
Cynthia's Turkey or Beef Tenderloin or Standing Rib Roast
Steamed Asparagus and Hollandaise Sauce
Grand Rice Pilaf • Pickled Peaches • Rich Egg Bread

DESSERT
Mock Egg Nog • Fruit Cake • Pear Mincemeat Pie

the spiritual renewal that can take place when we appreciate the gifts God has given us. Allow the meal, with its many delightful aromas, temperatures, tastes, appearances, and textures, to be an expression of God's abundant provision for us all.

HOT BRIE

This recipe is exciting to serve at Christmas because all of the ingredients were commonly used, in one form or another, during the time of Christ's birth. Milk products, almonds, and honey were each nutritional staples from the time of the patriarchs. Cheese in particular was an important part of a person's diet and was often given as a gift.

6" or 8" round of brie   ½ cup sliced almonds
½ stick softened butter   2 or 3 tablespoons honey

Preheat oven to 300°. Place brie in a well-oiled baking dish. Spread softened butter over top of cheese. Scatter almonds over butter. Bake until cheese softens. Remove brie from oven before cheese splits through the rind. Drizzle honey over the top and serve.

Serve melba toast to dip into cheese. It is sturdy and won't add a distracting flavor to the dish.

SCALLOPED OYSTERS

Since some people don't like oysters, you may substitute scallops, or divide the recipe with half of each.

5 cups oysters, soda cracker crumbs, and paprika

SAUCE:

5 tablespoons butter	*2 beaten eggs*
5 tablespoons flour	*½ teaspoon salt*
2 cups whole milk, hot	*½ teaspoon white pepper*

TWENTY-FOUR-HOUR SALAD

A popular feature of Jewish feasts was a sauce made of vinegar and fruits. This is a contemporary version of that ancient recipe.

1 cup whipped cream	*DRESSING:*
2 cups chunk pineapple	*4 tablespoons vinegar*
2 cups cherries	*4 tablespoons sugar*
2 cups marshmallows	*2 eggs*
2 cups fresh orange slices	*2 tablespoons butter*

Combine vinegar, sugar, eggs, and butter in double boiler. Warm over medium-low heat until thick. Cool mixture. Add whipped cream. Mix with fruit and let stand in refrigerator for 24 hours to let dressing soak into fruit.

ARTICHOKE PARMESAN

A key ingredient in this recipe, dill weed, was one of the most common spices used in biblical times.

2 cans artichoke hearts
½ cup mayonnaise
½ cup fresh grated Parmesan
⅛ teaspoon dill weed
⅛ teaspoon garlic salt
(Ingredients may be varied to accommodate personal tastes.)

Preheat oven to 325°. Drain and chop artichoke hearts. Stir in mayonnaise and Parmesan until the texture pleases you. Add seasonings. Spoon mixture into a lightly greased casserole dish. Bake for 15-20 minutes in the top third of oven, until top is brown. Serve with melba toast or crackers. Rinse oysters carefully, checking for bits of shell. Drain them on fresh cotton kitchen towels. While they are draining, make the sauce.

Melt butter in medium saucepan, then add flour, stirring until thoroughly mixed. Cook over medium-low heat, stirring constantly for one minute. Add hot milk and continue stirring. When sauce has thickened, remove from heat and let cool.

Beat eggs and add salt and pepper. Check sauce. When it is cool enough that eggs will not set, stir eggs into it.

Place oysters in oiled baking dish. Pour warm sauce over them. Scatter cracker crumbs evenly over mixture. Dust with paprika. Bake at 300° on the top rack of oven until barely set and slightly brown.

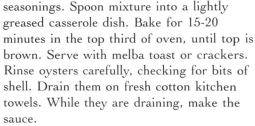

CYNTHIA'S TURKEY

Desert game was served often in ancient times. My favorite holiday meat is turkey. I have created a special marinade that brings out this meat's wonderful flavor.

1 whole turkey

MARINADE:
Juice of 2 lemons
4 teaspoons paprika
2 teaspoons each
   fresh crushed garlic,
   curry powder,
   Cavender's seasoning
½ cup olive oil
3 tablespoons honey

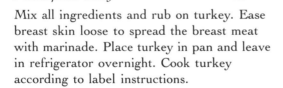

Mix all ingredients and rub on turkey. Ease breast skin loose to spread the breast meat with marinade. Place turkey in pan and leave in refrigerator overnight. Cook turkey according to label instructions.

BEEF TENDERLOIN

Beef was a particularly rare dish in ancient times and was served on only the most special occasions to only the most honored of guests. I can't think of a more "special" occasion than Christmas, and I frequently offer our "honored guests" my personal version of the fatted calf.

Rub tenderloin with olive oil, salt, pepper, garlic, and soy sauce. Let stand in bowl for one hour before roasting.

Preheat oven to 450°. Roast for approximately one hour. Remove tenderloin from oven and insert meat thermometer until tip reaches center. Reduce heat to 350° and roast until thermometer registers 140°.

Serve with horseradish sauce (below).

HORSERADISH SAUCE:
½ pint whipping cream
3 tablespoons minced horseradish
2 tablespoons Dijon mustard
salt to taste

Whip cream and then add other ingredients. Serve on the side.

STANDING RIB ROAST

One of the key ingredients in this dish is garlic. Garlic was a very popular spice in ancient Egypt and was no doubt one of the luxuries the Israelites missed during their wilderness trek.

Rub rib roast with salt, pepper, and garlic powder. Let stand at room temperature for one hour. Place rib roast side down in a roasting pan. Put in a cold oven and turn temperature to 375°.

Cook for one hour. Turn oven off, keeping oven door closed. Approximately 30 minutes before you plan to eat dinner, turn oven to 375° again and resume cooking. Remove roast just before serving.

GRAND RICE PILAF

This marvelous concoction is a classic example of how the most common of ingredients can become a culinary masterpiece. Despite its simplicity, you may wish to attempt a "dress rehearsal" for some willing friends before you serve it at your Christmas celebration.

3 cups long-cooking rice
6½ cups chicken or turkey stock
4 tablespoons garlic butter
3 tablespoons olive oil
2 green bell peppers, sliced in thin strips
12 green onions, chopped
4 ribs celery, sliced the same thickness as pepper
8 ounces fresh mushrooms, sliced
2 carrots, sliced into 1" long thin strips

6 ounces dried apricots, cut into 1" long strips
½ cup golden raisins
4 ounces slivered almonds (toasted sesame seeds or sunflower seeds may be substituted)
Salt to taste
Chopped parsley for garnish

Cook rice in chicken or turkey stock according to the directions for the brand of rice you purchase. Mix garlic butter and oil together and sauté vegetables until slightly crisp. Shape cooked rice into a design that reflects your Christmas theme. Gently pour warm vegetables over the rice so as not to lose the design you have created. Add the fruits, nuts, and parsley as a festive garnish.

STEAMED ASPARAGUS AND HOLLANDAISE SAUCE

During the Old Testament period, eggs — particularly egg whites — were sometimes used as a symbol for something bland and uninteresting. I think you'll agree, though, that there is nothing bland about this recipe.

3 egg yolks
1 cup melted butter
1 tablespoon lemon juice
Fresh asparagus, steamed

As you steam asparagus, slowly stir other ingredients together in another pan over very low heat. When mixture has warmed and thickened, pour over steamed asparagus.

PICKLED PEACHES (canning recipe)

For many years, my husband's family has owned a summer home in the hills of Arkansas, at a place called Mt. Nebo. This delightful spot has served as a spiritual retreat, a place for family gatherings . . . and a source of some of the best peaches I have ever tasted!

Although we prepare this delicious treat in August when the peaches are at their juiciest, we always save at least one jar for our Christmas feast to remind us of the many good times we shared during the previous months. Next summer, whether from a grocer or from your own orchard, try canning a batch of these golden tributes to warm, lazy days. Then, when you gather for your Christmas feast, they will be more than just a tasty dish — they will become an adventure of memories.

1 peck (16 lbs.) of
*   peaches (preferably*
*   Clingstone variety)*
1 box cloves (enough
*   for two to three*
*   cloves per peach)*

SYRUP:
4 cups vinegar
7 cups sugar
6 2-inch sticks of
*   cinnamon*

Peel the peaches, then insert two or three cloves in each peach. Set peaches aside and prepare the syrup. Combine vinegar and sugar in a large saucepan. Heat at medium temperature, stirring constantly, until sugar dissolves. Add cinnamon to syrup, then add enough peaches to fill a quart jar. Heat peaches thoroughly until fork-tender (approximately 1-2 minutes), then place just the peaches (no syrup) in a quart jar. Continue this process until all the peaches have been jarred. Then boil the syrup for a few more minutes and pour over the peaches. Seal the jars immediately.

RICH EGG BREAD

Bread was a very common food in ancient times. As you enjoy one of these delightful buttered rolls, try to think of ways in which you can make our Savior, Jesus Christ — the One referred to in Scripture as the Bread of Life — common to our hungry world.

1 cup milk, scalded and cooled
1 stick butter or margarine
½ cup sugar
1 teaspoon salt
2 eggs
1 package yeast, dissolved in ¼ cup warm water
3 cups flour

Mix together scalded milk, butter, sugar, and salt. Let mixture cool, then add eggs, dissolved yeast, and 1½ cups flour, stirring each ingredient in thoroughly before adding the next. Beat mixture well. Place mixture in lightly oiled bowl and cover with a damp cloth. Allow to rise one hour. Thoroughly remix dough by hand or mixer, adding remaining 1½ cups flour. Cover with towel and place in refrigerator overnight.

Approximately 2½ hours before your meal, separate dough into large balls and place in a well-greased pan. Melt one stick of butter and pour over dough balls. Cover and let rise for 2 hours.

Preheat oven to 375°. Bake for 30 minutes.

MOCK EGG NOG

1 cup milk   *1 teaspoon vanilla*
2 eggs   *½ pint whipping cream*
¼ cup sugar   *Vanilla ice cream*

Heat milk to near boiling point and then reduce heat. Beat eggs and sugar together and add to hot milk, mixing continuously. Cook over low heat until mixture coats mixing spoon. Remove from heat and allow mixture to cool. Add vanilla and whipping cream. When ready to serve, add one scoop vanilla ice cream to each cup of egg nog.

PEAR MINCEMEAT PIE

When I make a pie filling, I like to make enough for more than one pie and freeze the rest. This recipe will yield filling for eight pies. (Use any standard pie crust recipe.)

7 pounds (4 quarts)   *1 cup grape juice*
   ground pears   *1 cup vinegar*
2 apples   *1 tablespoon cinnamon*
2 oranges   *1 tablespoon allspice*
2 lemons   *1 tablespoon cloves*
1 pound raisins   *1 tablespoon nutmeg*
2 cups currants   *1 tablespoon salt*
6 cups sugar

Grind together the first six ingredients (the fruits). Mix in remaining ingredients. Cook over a low heat, uncovered, for 2 hours. Allow mixture to cool, then place in one-pint freezer containers and freeze. Before baking a pie, you may add fresh nuts or fruits as desired.

FRUIT CAKE

Although the fruit cake has been mocked and ridiculed in recent years, its festive appearance makes it a perfect holiday centerpiece, and its distinct taste will top off any meal.

½ pound each of diced red candied cherries,
   green candied cherries, red candied pineapple,
   green candied pineapple
½ pound coconut
1½ pounds pecans
1 can condensed milk
1 teaspoon vanilla
1 pound diced dates

Mix all ingredients and pack in a large greased pan. Preheat oven to 200° and bake for 2 hours. Cool cake completely before removing from pan.

THREE

A Gift of
Worship

My Father is a pastor. Perhaps because the meaning of the season is so dear to him, some of his finest and most inspiring messages have been delivered at Christmas. I have woven together into a brief sermonette a collection of some of his most memorable thoughts from past years.

I hope you will take time out this Christmas to attend a candlelight service at a local church. God has given us so much through his Son. Let us gratefully offer him the gift of our worship and adoration during this holy season.

Mary responded, "Oh, how I praise the Lord. How I rejoice in God my Savior! For he took notice of his lowly servant girl, and now generation after generation forever shall call me blest of God. For he, the mighty Holy One, has done great things to me. His mercy goes on from generation to generation, to all who reverence him."
(Luke 1:46-50)

Listen. Be quiet for a moment. Now for just a moment longer. It's hard, isn't it? It's difficult in a noisy, frantic, and sometimes bewildering culture to stop for a few minutes and contemplate something deeper than whether our shoes match our slacks as well in the daylight as they did in a half-lit bedroom.

Actually, I don't believe there has ever been a time when solitude and reflection were regular features of everyone's day. It's almost impossible to find a moment in history when there weren't such distractions as war, famine, and pestilence.

This is why the people described in the Gospel accounts of our Savior's birth are so remarkable. Jesus was born into one of the most chaotic times and places in history. Yet we are told that God's people were willing to stop, listen, and act upon the incredible things they were told.

Consider Elizabeth, who believed God would fulfill the promise he gave her husband Zacharias that she would bear a child. As a result, Elizabeth is pictured in Scripture as a woman tremendously blessed by the Lord.

The shepherds to whom the hosts of heaven announced the birth of the Christ child left their flocks of sheep and went by faith to a manger in Bethlehem to worship and praise God. Visiting wise men took heavenly counsel and returned home — ignoring the command of an earthly king to report back when they found the baby.

The most praiseworthy examples of devotion and obedience can be seen in the lives of the man and woman chosen to be the Messiah's parents: Mary and Joseph. Rather than making expedient or sensible decisions, they followed the guidance of the Holy Spirit. Instead of being proud and boastful of the honor they had been given, they were humbled by the Lord's generosity.

Each Christmas I try to model my holiday activities after the lives of these godly people. If we do not devote time each Christmas to listening for the voice of God and seeking his guidance, then we are missing the greatest joy this holy season can bring.

The Lord has graciously spoken to me during my holiday times of quiet meditation. One wonderful insight he gave me was an understanding of how we should try to minister through the commercialism that has become part of the Christmas season. As distorted as the message might be, it is the closest many people come to hearing about Christ. Instead of condemning others for not honoring the spiritual significance of Christmas, we need to use these presentations as opportunities to share with people the true meaning of this blessed season.

Also, "Peace on Earth" is something more than a nice phrase in a greeting card. Christmas is a time to seek peace, and sometimes forgiveness, with others. It is probably the best time of year to resolve conflicts and heal broken relationships. There is no greater gift you can give yourself than a restored relationship.

Finally, we need to spend less time each Christmas giving away presents and more time giving away ourselves. Sometimes I think we believe that moral and financial support of charity organizations and missions is sufficient for accomplishing Christ's mandate to be servants of those around us. Only when we stop holding on to those things that are meaningless and give away that which has meaning will we ever truly understand what Christmas is about.

This holiday season, let God's light shine in you and decorate your Christmas. Allow him to speak to you in the quiet moments. Experience in a new, marvelous way the wonder and joy felt by those who first experienced our Lord's presence.

A Gift of Peace

One of the most beautiful pieces of literature in the English language is St. Luke's account of our Savior's birth as recorded in the King James Version of the Bible. No musical composition, work of art, or devotional text has so captured the majesty and the significance of Christ's entrance into his earthly kingdom.

In the early church the Word of God was read aloud to edify the believers. I sometimes think we don't place enough emphasis on the wisdom and power that comes from simply reading and hearing the truth of Scripture.

As you read the following words, say them slowly, savoring their meaning. After you read, offer a prayer of thanksgiving for the blessings God has given us in his Son. Ask God to open the heart of each person in the room so that the Holy Spirit can speak to him or her. Close by allowing anyone who wishes to share what the story you have just read means to him or her.

As you establish family Christmas traditions, make this time of spiritual renewal the center of your activities. You will be setting an appropriate tone for the entire season, and you will experience a peace that will remain with you always.

Luke 2:1-20   *And it came to pass in those days, that there went out a decree from Caesar Augustus, that all the world should be taxed. (And this taxing was first made when Cyrenius was governor of Syria.) And all went to be taxed, every one into his own city. And Joseph also went up from Galilee, out of the city of Nazareth, into Judaea, unto the city of David, which is called Bethlehem; (because he was of the house and lineage of David:) To be taxed with Mary his espoused wife, being great with child.*

And so it was, that, while they were there, the days were accomplished that she should be delivered. And she brought forth her firstborn son, and wrapped him in swaddling clothes, and laid him in a manger; because there was no room for them in the inn.

And there were in the same country shepherds abiding in the field, keeping watch over their flock by night. And, lo, the angel of the Lord came upon them, and the glory of the Lord shone round about them: and they were sore afraid. And the angel said unto them, Fear not: for, behold, I bring you good tidings of great joy, which shall be to all people. For unto you is born this day in the city of David a Saviour, which is Christ the Lord. And this shall be a sign unto you; Ye shall find the babe wrapped in swaddling clothes, lying in a manger.

And suddenly there was with the angel a multitude of the heavenly host praising God, and saying, Glory to God in the highest, and on earth peace, good will toward men.

And it came to pass, as the angels were gone away from them into heaven, the shepherds said one to another, Let us now go even unto Bethlehem, and see this thing which is come to pass, which the Lord hath made known unto us.

And they came with haste, and found Mary, and Joseph, and the babe lying in a manger. And when they had seen it, they made known abroad the saying which was told them concerning this child. And all they that heard it wondered at those things which were told them by the shepherds.

But Mary kept all these things, and pondered them in her heart. And the shepherds returned, glorifying and praising God for all the things that they had heard and seen, as it was told unto them.

FOUR

A Gift of Praise

FROM SOLOMON to John Milton to T. S. Eliot, some of God's most gifted and earnest believers have used verse as a vehicle of praise to their Creator. In fact, when he was twelve years old, my nephew Matthew Wright demonstrated that age dictates neither talent nor devotion with the following poems:

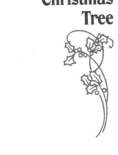

The Christmas Tree

Oh, what a sight is the Christmas tree,
The wreath upon the door,
The lights!
They are something to see.
And the presents on the floor. . . .
But if I base my Christmas on these things,
Like so many others do,
I'll miss the true meaning of Christmas,
And probably my joy, too!

Millions, thousands, hundreds, tens;
All come blowing in the wind.
Some come in circles, some come with spikes.
They're wonderfully made
They're glistening white.
Flying like angels through the air,
With wings like the dove,
They float here and there.
They cover the ground with a blanket of white,
They sparkle, they glisten,
Reflecting pale moonlight.
What is this sensation,
Of God's creation?
Surely you know,
Its name is snow!

White Wings

I, too, love to write poetry, but generally I use my stanzas and couplets as lyrics in my music.

While I know that music is the calling to which God has asked me to devote my life, I sometimes think that the words I labor and pray so hard over are not heard with the same intensity as I felt when I composed them. Thus, in this final chapter, I want to add my own offering of praise to this collection, and present my poetry in a format that requires your voice and not mine.

I thank you for allowing me to share some of my memories with you, and I hope your family will find the peace and joy that is our inheritance as Christians during this blessed season. And, of course, I hope that all of your Christmases are white!

It's the Thought

And a loving thought sends us out to find,
Something special for someone on our mind,
And we think of friends and our family,
As we hang our gifts on the Christmas tree.

It's the thought that counts, when the thought is love,
It's the thought that counts, when you're thinking of
How the money flows in vast amounts,
When the thought is love, it's the thought that counts.

And a loving thought sent a snow-white Lamb,
To a little town known as Bethlehem,
And the little Lamb thought of you and me,
As He hung His gift on the Christmas tree.

It's the thought that counts, when the thought is love,
It's the thought that counts, when you're thinking of
His blood that flowed in vast amounts;
When the thought is love, it's the thought that counts.

Wandering pilgrim, searching alone;
Weary from travel, so far from home.
You need a firelight inside you to guide you;
Oh, wandering pilgrim, look to the wonderful Star.

Wandering pilgrim, please take my hand;
I've been a pilgrim, I know the land.
You need an escort beside you to guide you;
Oh, wandering pilgrim, look to the wonderful Star.

Wandering pilgrim, be not afraid;
There is the sign in heaven displayed.
You need a Savior inside you to guide you;
Oh, wandering pilgrim, look to the wonderful Star.

Please let me show you the Star,
Follow that wonderful Star.

Wandering Pilgrim

Alleluia, Christ Is Born

Shepherds adore Him, kneeling before Him,
Alleluia, Christ is born.
With holy voices,
Heaven rejoices,
Alleluia, Christ is born.
This humble station bringing salvation,
To every nation forever.
Lift up your eyes and follow the wise men,
Alleluia, Christ is born.
Offer your treasure, seeking His pleasure,
Alleluia, Christ is born.
Evil restraining, power attaining,
Ruling and reigning forever.
Alleluia, Christ is born.
Carol the story, singing His glory,
Alleluia, Christ is born.

Lamb of God

Your only Son, no sin to hide,
But You have sent Him from Your side,
To walk upon this guilty sod,
And to become the Lamb of God.

Your gift of Love they crucified,
They laughed and scorned Him as He died,
The humble King they named a fraud,
And sacrificed the Lamb of God.

Oh, Lamb of God, sweet Lamb of God,
I love the Holy Lamb of God,
Oh, wash me in His precious blood,
My Jesus Christ, the Lamb of God.

I was so lost, I should have died,
But You have brought me to Your side,
To be led by Your staff and rod,
And to be called a lamb of God.

Oh, Lamb of God, sweet Lamb of God,
I love the Holy Lamb of God,
Oh, wash me in His precious blood,
Till I am just a lamb of God.

Oh, wash me in His precious blood,
My Jesus Christ, the Lamb of God.

It All Goes Back

We're given more than we could earn,
A carryover from the past.
But are we able to discern,
The source of legacy amassed?
Heritage is free through a family servant dynasty,
Servant dynasty,
It is beautiful to me.

And it all goes back to You,
Anything I do.
I know enough to know I'm nothing on my own,
It all goes back to You.
I know where I began, I owe You what I am,
It all goes back to You.

We are the planting of our Lord,
The painful labor of Your hand,
Only to You is the reward,
For living roots on which we stand.
Heritage is free through a family,
Evergreen,
Indeed, it is beautiful to me.

And it all goes back to You,
Anything I do.
I know enough to know I'm nothing on my own,
It all goes back to You.
I know where I began, I owe You what I am,
It all goes back to You.

Runner

Courier valiant, bearing the flame;
Messenger noble, sent in His name;
Faster and harder, run through the night;
Desperate relay, carry the light.

Obstacle ancient, chilling the way;
Enemy wakened, stoking the fray;
Still be determined, fearless and true;
Lift high the standard, carry it through.

Runner, when the road is long;
Feel like giving in, but you're hanging on;
Oh, Runner, when the race is won,
You will run into His arms.

Mindful of many, waiting to run;
Destined to finish, what you've begun;
Millions before you, cheering you on;
Godspeed, dear runner, carry it home.

Runner, when the road is long;
Feel like giving in, but you're hanging on;
Oh, Runner, when the race is won,
You will run into His arms.